The Journey to
MAX

An adoption story

By Christopher & Alejandro Garcia-Halenar

**Special thanks to Robert, Jackie and the entire team
at Advocates for Children and Families
for helping us find our unicorn.**

The Journey to Max – An Adoption Story
Copyright © 2021 by Christopher and Alejandro Garcia-Halenar
All rights reserved.

ISBN-13: 978-1-7326044-2-1
Illustrations by: Lea Embeli

Published by:
XanMaxBooks
www.xanmaxbooks.com

Printed in the United States.

When we least expected,
hope peeked his little head into our lives –
like a tiny storm of joy and happiness.

MY NAME IS XANDER,
THIS IS MY LITTLE BROTHER

MAX.

WE LIVE WITH OUR TWO DADS

AND OUR FAITHFUL DOG, SHELBY.

I LOVE
VIDEO GAMES.

MAX LOVES MUSIC.

AND OUR DADS?
THEY LOVE US.

FOR A LONG TIME WE WERE JUST THREE.

OUR HEARTS NEVER REACHED A FULL BEAT.

IN THE BACK SEAT OF THE CAR,
I ALWAYS RODE ALONE.

I HAD A ROOM FULL OF TOYS
BUT NO ONE TO PLAY WITH.

AT RESTAURANTS,
THERE WAS ALWAYS
AN EMPTY CHAIR.

THEN MAX ARRIVED.

THIS IS THE STORY OF HOW
WE FOUND EACH OTHER.

FINDING MAX WAS A LOT OF WORK.
EACH TRIP STARTED
OUT HOPEFUL.

NO MATTER HOW FAR
WE SEARCHED,

WE RETURNED HOME WITHOUT HIM.

IT MADE US SAD.

GROWING OUR FAMILY
SEEMED IMPOSSIBLE.
WHAT WE DIDN'T
KNOW...

MAX ALREADY STARTED HIS JOURNEY TO FIND US.

Only miles from our house,
a kind, brave, and beautiful, young woman
struggled with a decision
that split her heart in two.

As much as she wanted to start a family, she knew this was not the right time, and

Max was already on his way.

SHE WAS DETERMINED TO FIND A FAMILY

WHO WOULD LOVE MAX AS MUCH AS SHE DID.

SHE WORKED HARD.

THEY HAD TO BE PERFECT FOR HIM.

JUST WHEN WE WERE READY TO GIVE UP,

She found us.
SHE CHOSE US!

I COULD NOT STOP SMILING.
IN TWO MONTHS I WOULD MEET
MY LITTLE BROTHER!

I HELPED DECORATE MAX'S ROOM.

I CHOSE MY FAVORITE
STUFFED ANIMAL FRIEND
TO MAKE HIM FEEL WELCOME
WHEN HE CAME HOME.

Our day came. He was here!
My stomach did somersaults waiting to meet him.
He was tiny — just over five pounds!

He was wrinkly
with squinty,
little eyes,
and smelled
kind of funny.

But I didn't care.
The empty spot
in my heart
wasn't empty anymore.

WHEN HE FIRST CAME HOME, HE DIDN'T DO MUCH –
JUST SLEEP AND DRINK HIS BOTTLE.

I HELPED FEED HIM,
THAT WAS COOL.

I GOT A NEW CHORE –
DIAPER DUTY.

LITTLE BABIES CAN REALLY STINK!

MAX GREW REALLY FAST.
SOON, HE WAS CRAWLING,

THEN WALKING,

AND RUNNING.

THAT'S WHEN LIFE GOT REALLY FUN!
WE CHASE EACH OTHER ALL OVER THE HOUSE.

SOMETIMES WE DO THINGS WE SHOULDN'T -
THAT'S WHEN WE GET IN TROUBLE.

OUR TIME-OUTS ALWAYS END WITH A HUG.

WE ARE LOVED.

When it comes to love,

Max is  SUPER loved.

He is loved by our dads and me,

our  Abuela

our huge extended family of

 Uncles  Aunts  Cousins

and he is loved by his  Birth Mom

Max and my parents
visit with his birth mom a couple times a year, and they check in on their phones a lot.

I'VE BEEN THINKING ABOUT YOU GUYS. I HOPE YOU ARE ALL DOING WELL.

HAPPY TWO MONTHS WITH MAXIMINO. I HOPE YOU ARE ALL DOING GREAT.

I'M GLAD HE'S ADAPTING WELL! I'M GLAD HE'S SUPER HEALTHY, IT MAKES ME HAPPY.

GOOD MORNING, I HOPE YOU ARE ALL DOING WELL. THANK YOU FOR THE BEAUTIFUL PICTURE OF MAX, IT MEANS SO MUCH TO ME. I'M SO HAPPY TO HAVE CHOSEN SUCH GREAT PARENTS FOR MAX.

MAKES ME SO HAPPY TO SEE MAX & XANDER BONDING.

HAPPY THANKSGIVING. I'M SO GRATEFUL FOR YOU GUYS. YOU HAVE NO IDEA HOW MUCH YOU MEAN TO ME. THANK YOU FOR EVERYTHING YOU'VE DONE. ALWAYS THINKING ABOUT YOU ALL.

Ever since he came home, she sends my dads texts and they send her pictures.

I LOVE OUR BIG, EXTENDED FAMILY.

MAX MAKES US SING LOUDER, LAUGH HARDER AND SMILE BRIGHTER.

Now the backseat is filled with laughter,

Toys are never lonely, and

Our table is always FULL!

Chris and Alex Garcia-Halenar are the proud fathers of their two sons, Xander and Max.

They live in the land of sunshine, dreams and hurricanes called South Florida.

They are firm believers that every child is unique and their story should be celebrated.

Their other celebratory works include the Award Winning Books,

"Xander's Story" - a Tale of Surrogacy, and

"The Adventures of Little Miss Crazy Hair - The Girl with Curl"

Lea Embeli is an illustrator from the beautiful country of Serbia. In 2017, she completed her undergraduate degree and her Master's in 2018. She has worked professionally since 2016, publishing several textbooks and children's picture books. She currently works as a freelance illustrator.

CPSIA information can be obtained
at www.ICGtesting.com
Printed in the USA
LVHW021937050122
707925LV00009B/500